The month of November, from the illuminated manuscript *Les Très Riches Heures du duc de Berry*

The Story of a Special Day
Volume 310

November

5

309th day of the year
(310th in leap years)
56 days remaining
until the end of the year.

by Michael Dobson

Timespinner
Press

This book is also available in e-book form for Kindle, e-pub devices, and other formats from your favorite online booksellers.

For more information about the series, about us, or about your special day, please email us at editor@timespinnerpress.com.

Look for other volumes in *The Story of a Special Day*, coming often. See www.timespinnerpress.com for details and for the most recent information.

Table of Contents

Cover: A Guy Fawkes Night celebration in 2010 (Photo: William Warby) — for the *Event of the Day.*

Back Cover and Frontispiece: The month of November, from the French Gothic illuminated manuscript *Les Très Riches Heures du duc de Berry.*

November 5 Quotations

"If ever I become entirely respectable I shall be quite sure that I have outlived myself."

 — *Eugene V. Debs, labor leader, born November 5, 1855*

"It may be true that you can't fool all the people all the time, but you can fool enough of them to rule a large country.""

 — *Will Durant, historian, born November 5, 1885*

"Thoughts are things; they have tremendous power. Thoughts of doubt and fear are pathways to failure. When you conquer negative attitudes of doubt and fear you conquer failure. Thoughts crystallize into habit and habit solidifies into circumstances."

 — *Bryan Adams, musician, born November 5, 1959*

"Records have images. There are wet records and dry records. And big records."

 — *Art Garfunkel, musician, born November 5, 1941*

"Laugh, and the world laughs with you; Weep, and you weep alone."

 — *Ella Wheeler Wilcox, poet, born November 5, 1850*

Event of the Day
The Gunpowder Plot

The Gunpowder Plot Conspirators

Remember remember the fifth of November
Gunpowder, treason and plot.
I see no reason why gunpowder, treason
Should ever be forgot...

On November 5, 1605, tipped off by an anonymous letter, British officials began a search of the House of Lords. Around midnight, they discovered a large stockpile of gunpowder — guarded by a man named Guy Fawkes.

Fawkes was a member of the Gunpowder Treason Plot, a plan to blow up the British House of

Lords and kill the King of England, so that the Protestant monarch would be replaced by a Catholic ruler.

Tensions between Catholics and Protestants in England had begun half a century before, when King Henry VIII split the English church away from Rome. Henry's daughter, Elizabeth I, persecuted English Catholics on the grounds that they were more loyal to Rome than to her. Elizabeth's conflict with her Catholic cousin, Mary Queen of Scots, ended with Mary's execution.

Elizabeth died childless and unmarried in 1603, and after some negotiation, the throne of England went to Mary's Protestant son, James VI of Scotland — who thereby became James I of England. Some Catholics had supported another candidate, but most were satisfied with James because his mother, after all, had been Catholic. And indeed, James was certainly more tolerant than had been Elizabeth. However, persecution of Catholics continued, and many Catholics were exiled.

Violence was all too common on both sides. Persecution of Catholics had the sanction of the State. Catholics, in turn, tried to assassinate several Protestant rules in both Europe and England, even making an attempt to poison Elizabeth.

Inevitably, plotters aimed at James. In the Buy Plot, two priests planned to imprison James in the Tower of London until he agreed to stop the persecution, but were talked out of it by their superiors in the church. Another plot aimed to kill James and his family so they could bring one of

James' Catholic cousins to the throne. In response to these plots, James ordered all Jesuits and Catholic priests to leave the country. Persecution raged anew — and in response, the most dangerous conspiracy of all came to be.

No longer content with imprisonment, the plotters decided to blow up the House of Lords during the State Opening. Most of the royal family would be present, as well as the Privy Council, the senior judges, most of the aristocracy, as well as senior members of the House of Commons. In one stroke, English government would be devastated, and the conspirators would install James' nine-year-old daughter and put her on the throne as a figurehead, with a Catholic nobleman as her official "protector."

The Gunpowder Plot had thirteen conspirators in all. The leader was Robert Catesby. Guy Fawkes himself was a soldier. Some say they got into the House of Lords by digging a tunnel from a nearby rented house, but no tunnel was ever found. But the plotters managed to bring in 36 barrels of gunpowder, enough for a titanic explosion. Fawkes would wait until the State Opening began, light the fuse, then escape across the Thames.

But an anonymous letter, sent to a Catholic noble urging him not to attend, unraveled the plot. The Catholic noble showed the letter to the king, and that triggered the search.

Guy Fawkes was tortured for two days until he finally broke and gave information on the other conspirators. Seven were arrested, tortured, convicted, and executed. The method of their death was drawing and quartering.

The Observance of 5th November Act passed Parliament in 1606, and for nearly two and a half centuries, Guy Fawkes commemorations were a feature of English life. Children traditionally made (and still make) "guys," effigies of Fawkes made of old clothes and a mask, to burn at the evening bonfire.

For a long time, the event had a distinctly anti-Catholic character, but today, the holiday is best known for bonfires and fireworks displays.

"Guy Fawkes in Ordall Cave," George Cruikshank

November 5 Holidays and Celebrations

Guy Fawkes Night (United Kingdom, New Zealand, Newfoundland)

An annual commemoration observed each November 5, Guy Fawkes Night is celebrated in the United Kingdom and some Commonwealth nations. It was celebrated in colonial North America as "Pope Day," focusing on its early anti-Catholic origins. Today, it is a secular celebration featuring bonfires and fireworks. It is also known as Bonfire Night.

West Country Carnival (England)

The West Country Carnival features a parade of illuminated floats, and the object of the evening is to raise money for local charities. Today, over 100 illuminated floats, each with as many as 22,000 lightbulbs, compete each year.

Kanakadasa Jayanthi (India)

Kanakadasa Jayanthi is a regional festival held in the Indian state of Karnataka (formerly Mysore), located in the south-west part of the country. The Kanakadasa Jayanthi celebrates the life and teachings of Kanaka Dasa (ಕನಕ ದಾಸ), a Hindu religious poet, philosopher, musician, and composer from the region.

West County Carnival float

Christian Feast Days

In *Western Christianity*, saints commemorated on November 5 include Domninus, Elizabeth the mother of John the Baptist, Galation, Magnus, and Pope Zachary.

In *Eastern Orthodox Christianity*, it is the commemoration of Saints Galacteon, Gaius of Ephesus, Philolgus of Sinope, and Pope Linus. (These are celebrated on November 18 by "Old Calendarists.)

What Happened on November 5?

1630 - **The St. Felix Flood**

On Saturday, November 5, 1530, a major flood in the Netherlands devastated the regions of Flanders and Zeeland. It is now known as "Evil Saturday."

1688 - **The Glorious Revolution Begins**

The Glorious Revolution deposed the last Catholic ruler of England and established the Hanoverian Succession under William and Mary.

When King James II and VII had a son would by his second (Catholic) wife, raising the possibility of a Catholic dynasty, a group of English nobles invited William of Orange, a Netherland prince who had married James II's Protestant daughter by a previous marriage, to take the throne.

With the support of a large portion of the English nobility, William crossed the English Channel with a large fleet. There were only two minor conflicts before James II fled the country. The new monarchs of England, William III and Mary II (generally known as William and Mary), came to the throne, ruling as co-monarchs. James II spent the remainder of his life in exile in France.

William and Mary

1757 - **Battle of Rossbach**

On November 5, 1757, the Prussian ruler Frederick the Great, defeated a large combined army of French and Austrians near the village of Roßbach, located in the Electorate of Saxony. Military historians consider Frederick's victory a masterpiece of strategy. Although outnumbered nearly two-to-one, Frederick's rapid movement allowed his forces to achieve nearly complete surprise, trapping the enemy before they could draw themselves up into battle formation, and devastated them. Frederick's army suffered only 550 casualties, while the enemy lost 10,000, with another 5,000 taken prisoner. This was an important battle in the Seven Years' War.

1763 - **Treaty of Fort Stanwix**

In North America, continued violence between the Iroquois nation and the British colonies led to this important treaty to establish new boundaries for the colonies. For a payment of £10,460 7s. 3d., the Iroquois agreed to settle claims with several states. The "Purchase" area of Pennsylvania takes its name from that settlement.

1831 - **Nat Turner is Convicted**

Nat Turner, a Virginia slave, led a rebellion against white plantation owners in August 1831. Sixty whites and over 100 blacks died in the unsuccessful rebellion. Rumors of widespread slave uprisings raged through the American South, and white militias and mobs killed many black slaves not involved in the rebellion — at least 200.

Turner was captured, tried, and sentenced to death on November 5, 1831. He was executed by hanging, along with 56 other accused slaves. In the aftermath of the rebellion, Virginia passed new laws prohibiting education and assembly rights for both slaves and free blacks, and requiring white ministers for black worship services.

Capture of Nat Turner

1872 - Susan B. Anthony is Arrested for Voting

On November 5, 1872, suffragist Susan B. Anthony (right) cast a vote in the 1872 Presidential election, claiming that the Fourteenth Amendment gave her the right to vote. Two weeks later, she was arrested for breaking the law.

Supreme Court Justice Ward Hunt personally presided over her trial in New York. He refused to allow her to testify on her own behalf, explicitly ordered the jury to find her guilty, and read an opinion from the bench that he had written before the trial had even started.

He imposed a fine of $100 dollars on her, but she refused. "I shall never pay a dollar of your unjust penalty," she said in court, and true to her word, she never did.

1895 - **First US Patent for an Automobile**

On November 5, 1895, patent lawyer and inventor George B. Selden (coincidentally the son of Henry Selden, the attorney who defended Susan B. Anthony), received the first patent for an automobile.

The actual Selden Road-Engine, a one-cylinder engine placed in a four-wheeled carriage, appeared in 1878. Sixteen years passed before the US Patent Office issued Patent 549160. Selden won a patent suit against Ford Motor Company, but Ford appealed and won. Selden's car company lasted until 1930, though Selden himself died in 1922.

1916 - **The Everett Massacre**

In Everett, Washington, shingle workers began a five-month strike, but local business owners paid vigilantes to beat the protesters with axe handles and run them out of town. To support their labor brothers, 300 members of the International Workers of the World (IWW, or "Wobblies") boarded two steamships on November 5, 1916, and headed to Everett. They were met at the docks by vigilantes led by law enforcement. A shot rang out, followed by a hail of gunfire. Most of the shooting came from the docks, though some Wobblies returned fire.

The death toll was five Wobblies and two "citizen deputies," along with numerous wounded. (The two dead deputies were shot in the back by their own side, not by IWW members on the ship.)

In spite of this, the IWW members conducted a protest march, and were arrested. The governor of Washington sent troops to restore order. All charges against the IWW members were subsequently dropped.

1925 - **The "Ace of Spies" is Executed**

Lieutenant Sidney George Reilly, known as the "Ace of Spies," was the first 20th century super spy, and the real-life model for Ian Fleming's character James Bond.

Working for the British Secret Service Bureau, Scotland Yard, and the Secret Intelligence Service, Reilly's daring exploits remain shrouded in mystery.

His most daring mission was an attempt to assassinate Vladimir Ilyich Lenin and overthrow the Bolshevik regime in Russia. The coup failed and Reilly fled the country. The Soviets tried him in absentia and sentenced him to death in 1918.

Reilly's subsequent exploits took him around the world. In 1925, undercover agents working for the Soviet secret police, the OGPU, lured Reilly back to Russia, supposedly to meet with an opposition group. It was a trap. Reilly was arrested, interrogated, and executed in accordance with the 1918 verdict against him.

The British TV series *Reilly: Ace of Spies*, was based on his life.

1990 - **Rabbi Meir Kahane Assassinated**

On November 5, 1990, Rabbi Meir Kahane (הרב
מאיר דוד כהנא), an American-Israeli rabbi known as
an ultra-nationalist, was assassinated in a Manhattan
hotel by El Sayyid Nosair, an Egyptian-born
American citizen, later convicted both for the
assassination and for his involvement in the 1993
World Trade Center bombing.

Kahane was a controversial figure. The Israeli
government had banned his political party Kach
("This is the Way") as racist and undemocratic. He
also founded the Jewish Defense League (JDL),
described as a "right-wing terrorist group" by the
FBI.

2005 - **Saddam Hussein Convicted**

On November 5, 2005, Iraqi dictator Saddam
Hussein (صدام حسين) and two of his associates,
intelligence chief Barzan Ibrahim al-Tikriti and chief
judge Awad Hamed al-Bandar were convicted and
sentenced to death.

The specific charge against Saddam and his
associates was the massacre of 148 Shi'a Iraqis that
had taken place in 1982, following an unsuccessful
assassination attempt against him.

While numerous observers, including Amnesty
International, condemned the trial as a kangaroo
court, the sentence stood, and Saddam was executed
by hanging on December 30, 2006.

Saddam Hussein at his trial

2009 - **Fort Hood Shooting**

On November 5, 2009, US Army Major Nidal Malik Hassan (نضال مالك حسن), a psychiatrist, attacked the most populous US military installation in the world, Fort Hood, located near Killeen, Texas. He killed 13 people and wounded 29 more in the worst shooting ever to take place on an American military base.

Who Was Born on November 5?

Artists

Jim Steranko (November 5, 1938 -)

A comic book legend whose most famous work is *Nick Fury: Agent of S.H.I.E.L.D.* for Marvel Comics. Steranko was named to the Will Eisner Comic Book Hall of Fame in 2006.

Cover of *Nick Fury, Agent of S.H.I.E.L.D.*, by Jim Steranko

Alton Tobey (November 5, 1914 - January 4, 2005)

A well-known muralist whose public art for the Depression-era Works Progress Administration can be seen at the Smithsonian and elsewhere, Tobey is also known for illustrating the 12-volume *Golden Book of American History*.

Richard Cosway (November 5, 1742 - July 4, 1821)

A leading portrait painter of the Regency Era, Cosway (self-portrait, right) was appointed the official painter to the Prince of Wales. His wife, Italian artist Maria Cosway, was a close friend of Thomas Jefferson.

Pietro Longhi (November 5, 1701 - May 8, 1785)

A Venetian painter who specialized in scenes of everyday life, Longhi also served as the Director of Venice's Academy of Drawing and Carving.

Musicians

Kevin Jonas (November 5, 1987 -)

Oldest member of the pop rock band the Jonas Brothers, he was named one of *People* magazine's Sexiest Men Alive in 2008.

Bryan Adams (November 5, 1959 -)

An award-winning composer, producer, and singer-songwriter, Bryan Adams has been nominated for 15 Grammys. *Billboard* named him 38th on the list of all-time top recording artists.

Peter Noone (November 5, 1947 -)

Best known as "Herman" from the 1960s rock group Herman's Hermits, Noone (right) is famous for hits such as "I'm Into Something Good," and "Mrs. Brown, You've Got a Lovely Daughter."

Gram Parsons (November 5, 1946 - September 19, 1973)

A singer, songwriter, guitarist and pianist, Parsons was a member of The Byrds and the Flying Burrito Brothers. He died at the age of 26 of a drug overdose.

Art Garfunkel (November 5, 1941 -)

Art Garfunkel is most famous as half of the folk-rock duo Simon & Garfunkel. As a solo artist, he had numerous hits in the top 40, and as an actor, received a Golden Globe nomination for his role in the movie *Carnal Knowledge*.

Art Garfunkel (right) with Paul Simon

Walter Gieseking (November 5, 1895 - October 26, 1956)

Gieseking's recordings of the complete solo piano works of Debussy, Mozart, and Ravel are critically praised.

Performers and Actors

Famke Janssen (November 5, 1965 -)

A Dutch actress and former model, Janssen is most famous for playing Bond bad girl Xenia Onatopp in *Goldeneye*, and Jean Gray/Phoenix in the *X-Men* movie franchise.

Tatum O'Neal (November 5, 1963 -)

Daughter of actor Ryan O'Neal, Tatum at age 10 became the youngest person to win a competitive Academy Award for her performance in *Paper Moon*.

Andrea McArdle (November 5, 1963 -)

Most famous for her Broadway starring role in *Annie*, Andrea McArdle (right) was the youngest person ever nominated for a Tony Award.

Tilda Swinton (November 5, 1960 -)

Swinton won an Academy Award in 2007 for her role in the movie *Michael Clayton*.

Robert Patrick (November 5, 1958 -)

A movie and TV actor most famous for his role as the villainous robot T-1000 in the movie *Terminator 2: Judgment Day*.

Jon-Erik Hexum (November 5, 1957 - October 18, 1984)

An American model and actor, he died in a firearms accident on the set of the CBS TV series *Cover Up*.

Kris Jenner (November 5, 1955 -)

Former wife of lawyer Robert Kardashian and current wife of athlete Bruce Jenner, Kris is best known as the matriarch of the Kardashian family of *Keeping Up With the Kardashians* and other reality television shows.

Armin Shimerman (November 5, 1949 -)

Actor best known for playing the Ferengi bartender Quark in *Star Trek: Deep Space Nine* and Principal Snyder in *Buffy the Vampire Slayer*.

Elke Sommer (November 5, 1940 -)

Actress and model known as a sex symbol in the 1960s, Sommer appeared in nearly 100 movies and TV shows as well as in several *Playboy* pictorials.

Vivien Leigh (November 5, 1913 - July 8, 1967)

Academy Award-winning actress Vivien Leigh is famous for playing Blanche DuBois in *A Streetcar Named Desire* and Scarlett O'Hara in *Gone With the Wind*.

Vivien Leigh

Roy Rogers (November 5, 1911 - July 6, 1998)

"King of the Cowboys," Roy Rogers appeared in over 100 movies as well as in a TV show, and was the most famous (and heavily marketed) cowboy star of his era.

Roy Rogers (left) with Mary Hart from *Shine on Harvest Moon*

Joel McCrea (November 5, 1905 - October 20, 1990)

Joel McCrea appeared in over 90 films during his career, including *Bird of Paradise* (controversial for a nude scene with Dolores del Rio), Alfred Hitchcock's *Foreign Correspondent*, and many more.

Politics and Government

Bob Barr (November 5, 1948 -)

A former Republican member of the House of Representatives from Georgia, Barr was one of the leaders of the impeachment of President Bill Clinton. He ran for President on the Libertarian ticket in 2008.

Cecil Underwood (November 5, 1922 - November 24, 2008)

Elected Governor of West Virginia twice (1957-1961 and 1997-2001), he was both the youngest and the oldest person ever to occupy that office. He was also the first guest on the TV game show *To Tell The Truth*.

Eugene V. Debs (November 5, 1855 - October 20, 1926)

A towering figure in the American labor movement, Debs was the Socialist Party candidate for President five times — the final time from prison, after speaking out against the World War I draft.

Science

Fred Lawrence Whipple (November 5, 1906 - August 30, 2004)

A leading American astronomer, Whipple developed the "dirty snowball" cometary hypothesis, and discovered numerous asteroids and comets.

J. B. S. Haldane (November 5, 1892 - December 1, 1964)

A pioneer in evolutionary genetics, Haldane is famous for the Briggs-Haldane Equation, and for mathematical treatments of natural selection. Haldane's Principle explains the relationship between the size of an organism and the bodily equipment it must have to function.

Léon Teisserenc de Bort (November 5, 1855 - January 2, 1913)

French meteorologist de Bort is famous for his discovery of the stratosphere, and for pioneering the use of unmanned instrumented balloons to explore the upper atmosphere.

Paul Sabatier (November 5, 1854 - August 14, 1941)

Paul Sabatier won the Nobel Prize for Chemistry in 1912 for discovering the Sabatier reaction, a method of recovering water from carbon dioxide with potential use on a future mission to Mars.

Words

Bernard-Henri Lévy (November 5, 1948 -)

A leading French intellectual and philosopher often referred to by his initials BHL. A founder of the New Philosophers School, Lévy is also famous for his investigation into the death of journalist Daniel Pearl.

Sam Shepard (November 5, 1948 -)

Pulitzer Prize-winning playwright and actor Sam Shepard received an Academy Award nomination for his portrayal of test pilot Chuck Yeager in *The Right Stuff*.

Will Durant (November 5, 1885 - November 7, 1981)

Author of the 10-volume *The Story of Civilization* and *The Story of Philosophy*, Durant received the Pulitzer Prize in 1968 and the Presidential Medal of Freedom in 1977.

Detail from *Le Jour ni l'Heure* by Maurice Utrillo

Who Died on November 5?

Artists

Al Capp (September 28, 1909 - November 5, 1979)

Al Capp was the writer and artist of the long-running American comic strip *Lil' Abner.*

Characters from *Lil' Abner* by Al Capp

Maurice Utrillo (December 26, 1883 - November 5, 1955)

A famous self-taught French painter of cityscapes, Utrillo was one of the few artists of Monmartre who was actually born there.

Musicians

Vladimir Horowitz (October 1 [O.S. September 18], 1903 - November 5, 1989)

Generally considered one of the greatest pianists of the 20th century, the Russian-American is best known for his performances of the Romantic piano repertoire.

Guy Lombardo (June 19, 1902 - November 5, 1977)

Guy Lombardo's Royal Canadians big band sold over 100 million records. They were billed as playing "the sweetest music this side of Heaven."

Art Tatum (October 13, 1909 - November 5, 1956)

Nearly blind since birth, Art Tatum (left, photograph by William P. Gottlieb) was widely acknowledged as one of the greatest jazz pianists of all time.

Performers and Actors

Jill Clayburgh (April 30, 1944 - November 5, 2010)

Actress Jill Clayburgh was nominated for Academy Awards for her movies *An Unmarried Woman* and *Starting Over.* She died of leukemia.

Fred MacMurray (August 30, 1908 - November 5, 1991)

Fred MacMurray starred in the 1944 film noir *Double Indemnity* and over 100 other movies. He is also known for the long-running television series *My Three Sons.*

Fred MacMurray

Jacques Tati (October 9, 1907 - November 5, 1982)

A French actor, writer, and director, Tati was named to *Entertainment Weekly's* list of the top directors of all time. His best known film in America is *Mr. Hulot's Holiday.*

Mack Sennett (January 17, 1880 - November 5, 1960)

Known as the "King of Comedy," director Mack Sennett pioneered slapstick comedy in film. His stable of stars included Charlie Chaplin, Bing Crosby, the Keystone Kops, the Keystone Bathing Beauties, and W. C. Fields.

Ward Bond (April 9, 1903 - November 5, 1960)

Ward Bond appeared in over 200 movies, primarily in supporting roles in Westerns and other adventure movies. He also starred in the long-running TV series *Wagon Train.*

George M. Cohan (July 3, 1878 - November 5, 1942)

The multitalented Cohan was a playwright, composer, lyricist, actor, singer, dancer, and producer, known as "the man who owned Broadway." The father of American musical comedy, his life and music form the basis of the film *Yankee Doodle Dandy* and the Broadway show *George M!*

Sheet music from the George M. Cohan musical *Little Nellie Kelly*, 1922.

Politics and Government

King Casimir III the Great (April 30, 1310 - November 5, 1370)

The only Polish monarch generally called "the Great," Casimir III inherited a ruined economy and war-devastated landscape, and through brilliant leadership, left Poland a wealthy and prosperous land. In addition to waging successful wars, Casimir III also reformed the Polish legal system and founded the Uniwersytet Jagielloński, commonly known as the University of Kraków.

Science

Alexis Carrel (June 28, 1873 - November 5, 1944)

A French surgeon who won the Nobel Prize in Physiology or Medicine for his pioneering work in vascular surgery, Carrel (working with Charles Lindbergh) developed the first perfusion pump, essential to open heart surgery. His views on eugenics and support of fascist policies remains controversial.

James Clerk Maxwell (June 13, 1831 - November 5, 1879)

Physicist James Clerk Maxwell formulated classical electromagnetic theory, which united electricity, magnetism, and optics into a unified system. Maxwell's equations are called the "second great unification in physics," the first being Isaac Newton's.

One of his other accomplishments, the Maxwell-Boltzmann Distributions, used statistical means to understand the kinetic theory of gases. Together, these ideas provided a foundation for special relativity and quantum theory.

Sports

Sam Jones (December 14, 1925 - November 5, 1971)

A Major League baseball player known as "Toothpick Sam" or "Sad Sam" Jones (right) started his career in the Negro Leagues. He joined the Cleveland Indians as a pitcher in 1951, and pitched

for a number of teams before his retirement in 1964. He was famous for his curveball, and for leading the National League in strikeouts and walks in three separate years. He was the first African-American in Major League baseball to pitch a no-hitter.

Words

John Fowles (March 31, 1926 - November 5, 2005)

English novelist and essayist John Fowles wrote *The Collector* and *The French Lieutenant's Woman,* both of which were made into movies, and *The Magus,* a mystical thriller. The London *Times* named Fowles one of the most important British writers of the last half of the twentieth century.

Lionel Trilling (July 4, 1905 - November 5, 1975)

Lionel Trilling was a member of the New York Intellectuals, a group of American writers and literary critics, a regular contributor to *The Partisan Review,* and generally considered one of the most important literary and cultural critics of the twentieth century.

The Month of November

When shrieked
The bleak November winds, and smote the woods,
And the brown fields were herbless, and the shades
That met above the merry rivulet
Were spoiled, I sought, I loved them still; they seemed
Like old companions in adversity.

William Cullen Bryant, A Winter Piece

The Eleventh Month

In Latin, *novem* means "nine," so it may seem strange that November is the eleventh month of the year. The original Roman calendar started in March, making November indeed the ninth month. No one is completely sure when the start of the year was moved to January, but the traditional name of November stuck.

In the northern hemisphere, November is a month in late autumn. In the southern hemisphere, November is in the springtime. May is its opposite month; spring in the north and fall in the south.

If it's not a Leap Year, November always starts on the same day of the week as February. If it is a leap year, November starts on the same day of the week as March.

November in Other Cultures

The month of November has different names in different languages. Some nations use calendars other than the Gregorian, and their months may overlap with November. Still, they often have a word for November itself.

Arabic: نوفمبر (Nūfambar)

Chinese and Japanese: 十一月

Croatian: Studeni
Czech and Polish: Listopad
Finnish: Marraskuu
Greek: Νοέμβριος
Hebrew: נובמבר
Hindi: नवंबर

Old English: Blōtmōnaþ
Russian: ноябрь

November Wedding Superstitions

"A November bride will be liberal and kind, but sometimes cold."

"Married in veils of November mist / Fortune your wedding ring has kissed."

"If you wed in bleak November, only joys will come, remember."

November Symbols

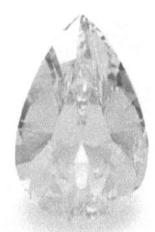

Birthstone Topaz (primarily yellow), and citrine (left).

Birth Flowers Chrysanthemum

Chrysanthemum

"Labors of the Month: November" by Simon Bening

November Events

Honorary Months

Presidents, Congresses, and nations around the world issue proclamations recognizing particular months to honor certain causes. These events generally fall in April. (All US unless otherwise noted.)

- Military Family Month
- National Hospice Month
- National Adoption Month
- National Family Caregivers Month
- National Alzheimer's Disease Awareness Month
- National Diabetes Month
- National American Indian Heritage Month
- Aviation History Month
- Child Safety Protection Month
- International Drum Month
- National Epilepsy Month
- National Model Railroad Month
- National Novel Writing Month
- Peanut Butter Lovers Month
- Real Jewelry Month
- National Sleep Comfort Month

Moveable and Multi-Day Events

Some events take place over a specific week or time period. Start and finish dates may vary from year to year. Some events occur on different days each year (such as "fourth Saturday of a month").

Election Day (United States)

Federal elections for President, Vice President, senators, and members of Congress in the United States are held on the Tuesday after the first Monday in November. Many state and local elections occur on the same day.

Melbourne Cup (Australia)

The Melbourne Cup is Australia's major thoroughbred horse race, known in Australia as "the race that stops a nation." It is held on the first Tuesday in November.

November Zodiac Signs

From the perspective of someone on Earth, the Sun appears to move through the sky throughout the year, along a path astronomers call the ecliptic plane. The ecliptic plane is divided into twelve constellations, known as the zodiac, based on traditionally observed patterns of stars. On your birthday, you can't see your constellation, because it's in the daytime sky.

The zodiac was first developed by Babylonian astronomers about 2,500 years ago. Because they were unaware that the Earth wobbles like a spinning top (known as *precession*), they didn't make allowance for the fact that the Sun's path through the zodiac changes over time.

That means there are now two sets of dates for your birth sign. The *tropical dates* are the original Babylonian dates; the *sidereal dates* tell you where the Sun actually appears as it moves along its annual path.

For November 5, the *tropical* sign is Scorpio, and the *sidereal* sign is Libra.

Scorpio

Tropical October 23 to November 21

Sidereal November 16 to December 15

Scorpio, the Scorpion, appears in the Greek myth of the hunter Orion. Because Orion had touched the robes of the goddess Artemis, in revenge, the goddess had the scorpion kill Orion. As a reward, she placed the scorpion in the sky, where it chases Orion through the eternal night.

Scorpio is a fire sign, and people born under this sign are supposed to be determined, reserved, loyal, and secretive. Scorpios are supposed to be compatible with the water signs of Pisces and Capricorn.

Libra

Tropical September 23 to October 23

Sidereal October 16 to November 15

The Babylonians considered Libra, the Scales, to be sacred to the sun god Shamash, patron of truth and justice. The Romans reassigned the scales to Astraea, the celestial virgin, better known as Virgo.

Libra is an air sign, and people born under this sign are supposed to be extroverts, socially graceful, and just. Librans are supposed to be compatible with the other air signs of Gemini and Aquarius.

Illustration by Edward Penfield

What Day of the Week is November 5?

On what day of the week does November 5 fall?

Surprisingly, this isn't an easy question. Because the calendar year is 365 days long (366 in leap years), it doesn't divide evenly by the seven days of the week.

Also, the Earth goes around the Sun in about 365-1/4 days, so a calendar tends to drift over time. That's why the same date falls on different weekdays in different years.

This is made even more complicated by a change in calendars that took place in 1582. Our modern calendar has its roots in ancient Rome, in a calendar reform conducted by Julius Caesar. Caesar commissioned mathematicians to attack the problem, and they came up with the idea of *leap years*, and thus standardized the calendar for centuries to come. This was called the *Julian calendar*.

Over time, however, the small errors in Caesar's calculation compounded. That's why Pope Gregory XIII commissioned the *Gregorian calendar*, used in most of the world today. Some countries converted in 1582, when the calendar was first developed; some converted later; other still haven't changed.

Gregorian and Julian aren't the only types of calendars. The Hebrew year, the Islamic year, and many other calendars are used in different parts of the world and among different people.

You can convert Gregorian dates to other calendars, including the Hebrew calendar, the Islamic calendar, and even the Mayan calendar by visiting the Fourmilab Calendar Converter at http://www.fourmilab.ch/documents/calendar/.

Chinese calendar systems are quite complex and have changed several times; a full discussion is far beyond the scope of this book. If you're interested, you can find information here: http://www.hermetic.ch/cal_stud/chinese_cal.htm.

A 50-year brass perpetual calendar.

Copyright, Credit, and Contact

Follow Us

Our blog *Dobson's Improbable History* (http://
improbhistory.blogspot.com) features short articles
on events and people associated with each day, and
updates several times each week. You can also get a
daily "What Happened In History" message and all
the latest Timespinner Press news by following us on
Facebook at https://www.facebook.com/
TimespinnerPress. Our Twitter feed
@SidewiseThinker links you to all our News of the
Day.

Contact Us

Find an error or a format problem? Want information
about the series, about us, or about when the volume
for your special day might be available? Please email
us at editor@timespinnerpress.com. (We also take
requests if your special day isn't yet complete. Please
give us at least six weeks' notice if possible.)

On Dates

Historians use "CE" (Common Era) and
"BCE" (Before the Common Era) instead of the more
common "AD" (*Anno Domini*, or Year of Our Lord)
and "BC" (Before Christ), reflecting the fact that the
year-numbering system established by the Gregorian
calendar is used throughout the world in many
countries not culturally Christian.

The CE/BCE designation dates back to at least
1708, and has been adopted as a standard by the
United Nations and the Universal Postal Union.
Because this series of books covers events and
people of all nations and cultures, we use the CE/
BCE terms.

The abbreviation "O.S." ("Old Style") on some
dates refers to the fact that the Russian Empire did
not switch from the Julian to the Gregorian calendar
at the same time as the rest of Europe, and therefore
some figures and events have two dates. (See "What
Day of the Week..." for an explanation of Julian and
Gregorian dates.)

People and events whose original names are not
in the Western alphabet have their native names
(where possible) in the appropriate script shown in
parenthesis. If you are using an e-reader to access an
electronic version of this book, all characters don't
always display on all devices.

Sources

We owe a great debt to Wikipedia, which is our first stop for research. We attempt to make independent confirmation of all important dates and facts through a variety of other sources. Other sources we frequently use include the Library of Congress; "on this day" listings from *Encyclopedia Britannica*, the New York *Times*, and the BBC; and, of course, the always essential Google.

All art and photographs are either in the public domain, used under a Creative Commons license, or with a "fair use" justification, and most frequently come from Wikimedia Commons and the Library of Congress Prints and Photographs Division.

Attribution is provided where requested by the copyright owner or when of historical significance, listed below. For information about any particular illustration or photograph, please contact us.

Credits

- The cover image of a Guy Fawkes wax model burning was taken in 2010 by William Warby, and is used here under CC-BY-SA 2.0.

- The illustration of the month of November used on the back cover and as the frontispiece is from the French Gothic illuminated manuscript *Les Très Riches Heures du duc de Berry* by the Limbourg Brothers, Jean Colombe, and an intermediate painter whose name is lost to history. It is in the public domain because its copyright has expired.

- The illustration of the Gunpowder Plot Conspirators is by an unknown artist, and is almost certainly from before 1923, and is thus in the public domain. The original is in the collection of the National Portrait Gallery, London. It has been cropped for use here.

- The illustration "Guy Fawkes in Ordsall Cave" is by George Cruikshank. It first appeared in William Harrison Ainsworth's *Guy Fawkes, or the Gunpowder Treason,* published in 1840. It is in the public domain because its copyright has expired. The image has been cropped and enhanced for its use here.

- The 1776 aquatint of a Windsor Castle Guy Fawkes Night celebration is by Paul Sandby. It is in the public domain because its copyright has expired.

- The 2006 photograph of the West County Carnival float "Samurai" was taken by "Trident13" and is used here under CC-BY-SA 2.5.

- The 18th century "Ceiling of the Painted Hall" was created by Sir James Thornhill. It has been cropped to show the detail of William and Mary. It is in the public domain because its copyright has expired.

- The woodcut engraving "Discovery of Nat Turner" appeared in the 1882 book *A Popular History of the United States.* It is in the public domain because its copyright has expired.

- The photograph of Susan B. Anthony was taken by Frances Benjamin Johnston between 1890 and 1906. It is in the public domain because its copyright has expired.

- The 2004 photograph of Saddam Hussein speaking during his trial is in the public domain as a work created by the US federal government.

- The cover of *Strange Tales Issue 167*, featuring "Nick Fury, Agent of S.H.I.E.L.D.," is copyright and trademarked by Marvel Comics. It is used here under "fair use" provisions of the copyright law to illustrate a biographical entry about the artist. Its resolution is too low to make it suitable for the production of counterfeit works and no comparable "free use" or public domain alternative exists. No challenge to either the copyright or trademark ownership is made or implied.

- The 1966 publicity photograph of Peter Noone from *The Danny Kaye Show* is in the public domain because it was published in the United States between 1923 and 1977 without a copyright notice. It has been cropped for its use in this book.

- The 1966 photograph of Simon & Garfunkel is from the Rijksfotoarchief in the Netherlands National Archives. It is used here under CC-BY-SA 3.0 Netherlands.

- The 1977 publicity photograph of Andrea McArdle as the lead character in the Broadway musical *Annie* is in the public domain because it was published in the United States between 1923 and 1977 without a copyright notice. It has been cropped for its use in this book.

- The MGM Studio publicity portrait of Vivien Leigh is in the public domain because it was published in the United States between 1923 and 1977 without a copyright notice.

- The 1938 publicity photograph of Roy Rogers and Mary Hart in the film *Shine on Harvest Moon* is in the public domain because it was published in the United States between 1923 and 1977 without a copyright notice.

- The photograph of Maurice Utrillo's *Le Jour ni l'Heure* was taken by Renaud Camus, and is used here under CC-BY-SA 2.0. The image has been cropped.

- The illustration of characters from the comic strip *Lil' Abner* is by All Capp, and is copyright and trademarked by Capp Enterprises. It is used here under "fair use" provisions of the copyright law to illustrate a biographical entry about the artist. Its resolution is too low to make it suitable for the production of counterfeit works and no comparable "free use" or public domain alternative exists. No challenge to either the copyright or trademark ownership is made or implied.

- The photograph of Art Tatum was taken by William P. Gottlieb between 1946 and 1948, and is part of the William P. Gottlieb Collection at the Library of Congress. By the wishes of the photographer, photographs in this collection entered into the public domain on February 26, 2010.

- The 1930s Paramount Pictures publicity photograph of Fred MacMurray is in the public domain because it was published in the United States between 1923 and 1977 without a copyright notice.

- The cover of *Little Nellie Kelly* sheet music by George M. Cohan was published by M. Witmark & Sons in 1922. It is in the public domain because its copyright has expired.

- The copyright status of the 1953 Topps baseball card of Sam Jones is unknown, and it is therefore assumed that the image is under copyright. It is used here under "fair use" provisions of the copyright law to illustrate a biographical entry about the artist. Its resolution is too low to make it suitable for the production of counterfeit works and no comparable "free use" or public domain alternative exists. No challenge to either the copyright or trademark ownership is made or implied.

- The photograph of a citrine is by Les Facettes and is used here under CC-BY-SA 3.0.

- The photograph of a chrysanthemum is by 池田正樹 (Masaki Ikeda). It was released into the public domain by its creator.

- The illustration of the month of May from *Hennessy Hours* is by Simon Bening, circa 1483/1484 — 1561. It is in the public domain because its copyright has expired.

- The cover of the November 4, 1922, issue of *Country Gentleman* magazine was painted by J. F. Kernan. It is in the public domain because its copyright has expired.

- The photograph of the 1906 automobile calendar by Edward Penfield is from the Library of Congress Prints and Photographs Division, and is in the public domain because it was published prior to January 1, 1923.

- The 50-year perpetual calendar photograph is in the public domain.

License Description and Terms

Aside from material purely in the public domain, photographs and other material in this book are used under specific licenses permitting free use, usually with attribution. For full text and terms of these licenses, click or enter the appropriate links below.

- Creative Commons Attribution 2.0 Generic (CC-BY 2.0): http://creativecommons.org/licenses/by/2.0/deed.en

- Creative Commons Attribution-Share Alike 3.0 Generic (CC-BY-SA 3.0): http://creativecommons.org/licenses/by-sa/3.0/

- Creative Commons Attribution-Share Alike 2.5 Generic (CC-BY-SA 2.5): http://creativecommons.org/licenses/by-sa/2.5/deed.en

- Creative Commons Attribution-Share Alike 2.0 Generic (CC-BY-SA 2.0): http://creativecommons.org/licenses/by/2.0/deed.en

- Creative Commons Attribution-Share Alike 1.0 Generic (CC-BY-SA 1.0): http://creativecommons.org/licenses/by-sa/1.0/deed.en

- CC0 1.0 Universal (CC0 1.0) Public Domain Dedication (CC0 1.0) http://creativecommons.org/publicdomain/zero/1.0/deed.en

- GNU Free Documentation License (GFDL): http://en.wikipedia.org/wiki/Wikipedia:Text_of_the_GNU_Free_Documentation_License

Timespinner
Press